VLAD

– AND THE –
GREAT FIRE OF LONDON
ACTIVITY BOOK

WRITTEN BY KATE CUNNINGHAM

ILLUSTRATED BY SAM CUNNINGHAM

Hi,

I'm Vlad the flea and this is my friend, Boxton the rat.

In September 1666 we were living in London having a wonderful time running around and biting things. That was until our night in Pudding Lane. We were there when the fire started and saw it all. There isn't much we don't know about what happened.

How about you? Let's see how much you know.

The Great Fire in numbers

Fleas aren't very good with numbers. Perhaps it's because we keep biting the teachers. Help me fill in the answers using the numbers at the side of the page.

On _____ September _____ a fire started in the bakery off Pudding Lane. It was _____ o'clock in the morning as the baker, Thomas Farriner and his family escaped from the flames.

The fire burned for _____ days, destroying around _____ of the City of London. _____ of people carried their belongings to the safety of the fields around London where they made shelters.

St Pauls Cathedral was burnt down during the fire. Sir Christopher Wren designed the new cathedral, but it was _____ years before it was completed in _____ .

1666

1710

2nd

one

three

forty-four

thousands

one third

Dot-to-Dot

Complete the dot-to-dot to see what Boxton
and I like to do best (after eating of course).
We were doing this in the bakery when the
fire started.

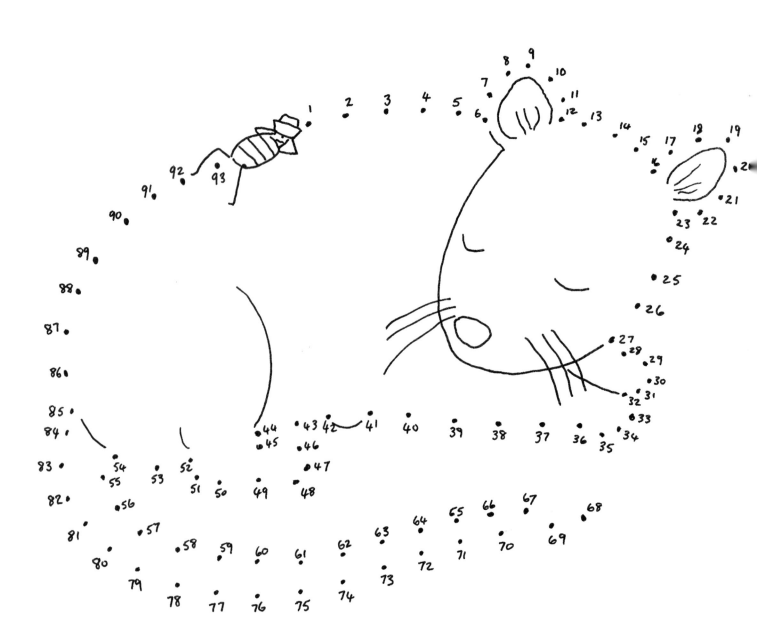

What's Wrong?

There's something wrong with this picture of the maid. Can you spot 5 mistakes and put a circle around each one?

Who am I?

These people seem a little muddled up. Perhaps if you unscramble the letters you will find out who they are.

"My people asked me to return and rule the country six years ago. They had had enough of those miserable puritans. I will not let this fire destroy our city, we will save and rebuild our city."

ngKi slarChe ll

"I work for the English Navy and keep an honest record of my life in my diary. No you can't see it, it is private! I have been to see the King and tell him about the danger of the spreading fire and he has ordered me to send messages to pull down houses to stop it."

Smelua sePpy

"I learnt my trade as an apprentice and now I have my own bakery. I have baked bread and cakes for the King. The fire wasn't my fault, it was someone else."

smoaTh reFriran

"My real job is as a blacksmith so I don't usually do this work. But when a fire breaks out I go to the hall to grab a fire hook and bucket and join the other volunteers, pulling down the buildings and collecting water to stop the fire destroying our homes."

threefigFir

The Duke of York has ordered us to march into the City of London with all this gunpowder from the Tower of London. We are going to blow up houses and make a gap in the buildings to stop the fire spreading. There's a lot more gunpowder back at the Tower, if the flames reach there the whole lot will explode and you would probably hear that in France!

drolieS

The Fire Game

Instructions for the Fire Game

The Aim: The winner is the first person to move their counter from Pudding Lane to Spitalfields.

Instructions:

Each player takes turns to roll the dice; the person with the highest score starts the game.

Starting on Pudding Lane, roll the dice and move your counter the number thrown.

The person on the left of the last player takes their turn to roll the dice and move.

If you land on a square with an instruction you need to follow the directions.

Continue to take turns clockwise around the players until one player reaches the final square and the safety of Spitalfields.

You will need: A dice (you can make one from the template on this page), one counter per player, the game board.

Dice template

Cut out around the outline, fold along the dotted lines. Glue the shaded flaps and stick on the inside of the cube.

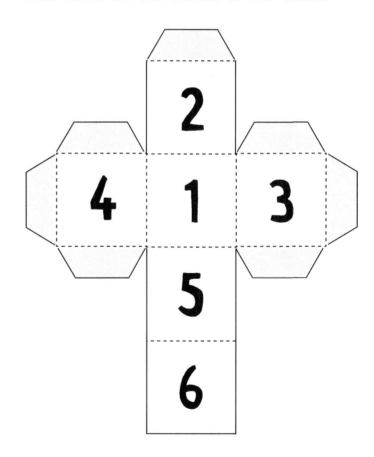

Counters

Fire Fact 1

Where did the Great Fire of London start?

a. Pye Corner

b. Pudding Lane

c. Apple Court

Well, this is a bit dull. Can you liven it up with some colour to show the effects of the fire?

Boxton is trapped!

Show him the way from Pudding Lane to the tents in Spitalfields. Quick before his tail gets singed!

By the way – there may be more than one way through the twisty streets, but you cannot go through gunpowder barrels or the flames.

Easy bread rolls

Ingredients:

225g (8 oz)	self-raising flour
15-25g (½ – 1 oz)	margarine
	milk
	pinch of salt

Method:

1. Heat the oven to 220°C / 425°F / gas mark 7.

2. Put the flour and salt into a bowl and mix.

3. Rub the margarine into the flour.

4. Add a little milk until the mixture sticks together.

5. Split the mixture into 6 equal pieces and shape into rolls.

6. Place on a baking tray and cook for 12-15 minutes.

7. Eat!

Acrostic

Use the clues to fill out this acrostic, putting the first letter in the grey column. When you have all the answers you can read a phrase vertically in the grey column.

1. — — — — — — — — —

2. — — —

3. — — — — — — —

4. — — —

5. — — — — — — — — — — —

6. — — — — — — — —

7. — — — — — —

8. — — — — — — —

9. — — — — —

10. — — — —

11. — — — —

12. — — — — — — — — — — —

13. — — — — — — — — —

14. — — — — —

15. — — — —

16. — — —

17. — — — — —

Clues:

1. A black powder that explodes when touched with fire. (9)

2. A rodent that looks like a mouse, but is bigger. Vlad's friend Boxton is one of these. (3)

3. The sound when something blows up, such as the answer to question 1. (9)

4. The soft grey powder left after something has been burnt. (3)

5. The name of the baker who owned the baker where the fire started. (6, 8)

6. A long tool used to pull down burning buildings when fighting the fire. (4, 4)

7. An intense, fierce fire. (7)

8. People who are forced to leave their homes because they are in danger. (8)

9. A small piece of glowing wood in a dying fire. (6)

10. A stove where you cook food. (4)

11. A tiny insect that jumps and feeds on blood. Vlad. (4)

12. A container used to carry water to the fire (7, 6)

13. The time when the fire started. (3, 1, 5)

14. After the sun has gone down. The opposite of day. (5)

15. Used to make walls in seventeenth century buildings: wattle and _ _ _ _ . (4)

16. The baker did not put his fire _ _ _ . (3)

17. The fire happened on this side of the River Thames. The opposite of south. (5)

Fire Wordsearch

I don't think you will find all these fire words.
They go across, up or down and diagonally.

y	i	g	y	l	i	c	g	b	p	a	d	d	r	o	u	h	c	e	s
n	r	u	b	z	i	h	l	d	s	u	z	e	p	e	f	f	t	f	b
x	u	m	o	n	s	m	o	u	l	d	e	r	n	s	d	i	a	e	l
u	w	l	y	p	h	u	w	m	m	z	j	n	o	u	h	v	c	x	a
s	x	x	c	m	f	f	v	p	o	j	t	w	y	w	h	o	x	k	z
i	l	y	p	f	l	a	m	m	a	b	l	e	l	s	h	r	r	x	e
q	u	y	l	v	i	m	n	n	l	g	c	i	i	w	b	a	s	g	s
o	u	a	g	l	l	n	q	q	i	x	c	a	v	t	l	n	y	d	c
q	r	o	k	c	t	r	m	q	g	t	t	q	s	i	n	g	e	p	t
e	b	l	v	r	z	n	l	o	h	p	r	g	b	u	e	e	a	c	p
v	w	e	m	b	e	r	s	l	t	g	r	o	e	d	m	v	v	q	w
q	t	u	x	i	d	k	l	s	i	s	v	m	s	n	f	z	i	u	k
n	n	x	n	t	s	i	x	e	b	d	k	n	c	q	l	r	x	r	i
b	m	z	f	l	i	c	k	e	r	w	w	p	f	h	a	s	h	l	i
k	u	r	r	a	n	n	h	c	y	c	i	o	i	f	m	f	o	e	n
d	m	m	n	x	q	h	g	r	u	m	j	y	a	b	e	l	l	s	f
h	m	a	e	t	q	y	h	u	b	t	d	x	j	r	s	m	o	k	e
v	w	p	m	p	g	o	u	d	i	p	w	z	j	u	c	y	u	x	r
a	o	g	l	o	t	u	l	s	p	s	x	g	g	z	q	i	n	o	n
w	o	l	l	e	y	n	n	t	i	z	h	i	f	r	e	o	f	u	o

- [ ] alight
- [ ] flammable
- [ ] singe
- [ ] ash
- [ ] flare
- [ ] smoke
- [ ] blaze
- [ ] flicker
- [ ] smoulder
- [ ] burn
- [ ] glow
- [ ] white
- [ ] embers
- [ ] inferno
- [ ] yellow
- [ ] extinguish
- [ ] orange
- [ ] flames
- [ ] red

Vlad the flea and Boxton the rat

1. Colour the puppets.

2. Cut around puppets and base. Carefully cut along the dotted line making sure not to cut across the middle where there is no line.

3. Bend the strip of paper under the dotted line around your finger and stick with glue or sellotape.

4. Use pink wool to add a tail to Boxton, the rat and black wool to add arms and legs to Vlad, the flea.

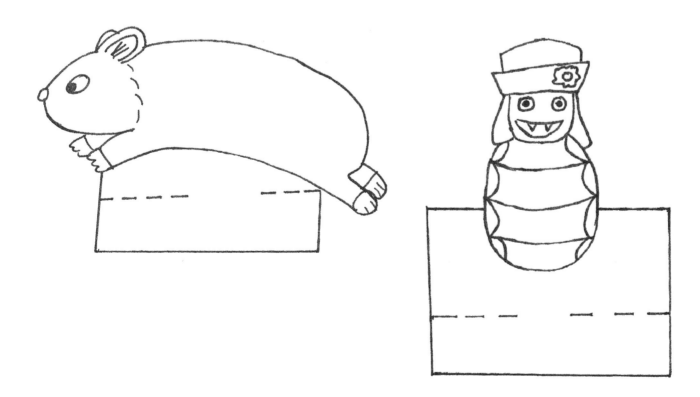

Fire Fact 2

What did Samuel Pepys bury in his garden in Seething Lane?

a. water and cake

b. beer and bread

c. wine and Parmesan cheese

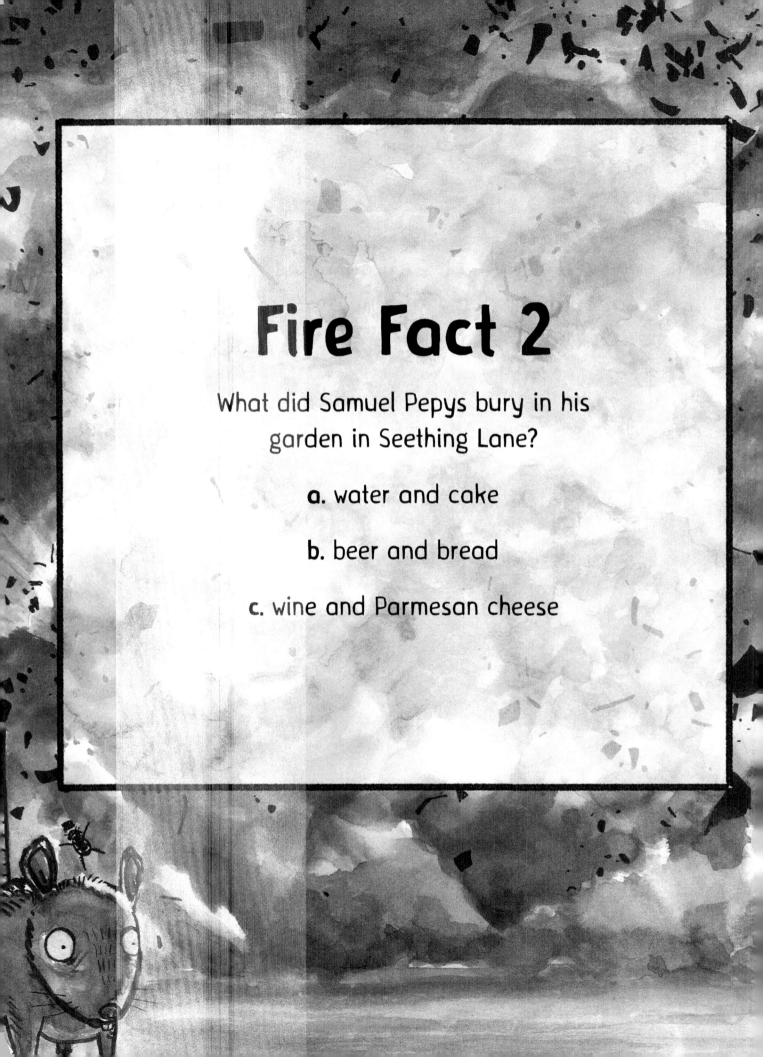

Londoners

fighting the Great Fire of London in 1666

1) Colour the puppets.

2) Cut around the outside of the puppets and bases.
Carefully cut along the dotted line making sure not
to cut across the middle where there is no line.

3) Put a blob of plasticine under the spots and
use a sharp pencil to poke a small hole through.

4) Use a split pin to attach the arms behind
the body of puppet.

5) Bend the strip of paper under the dotted line
around your finger and stick with glue or sellotape.

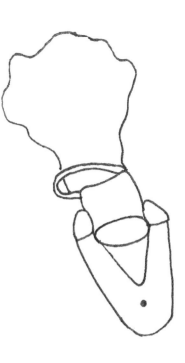

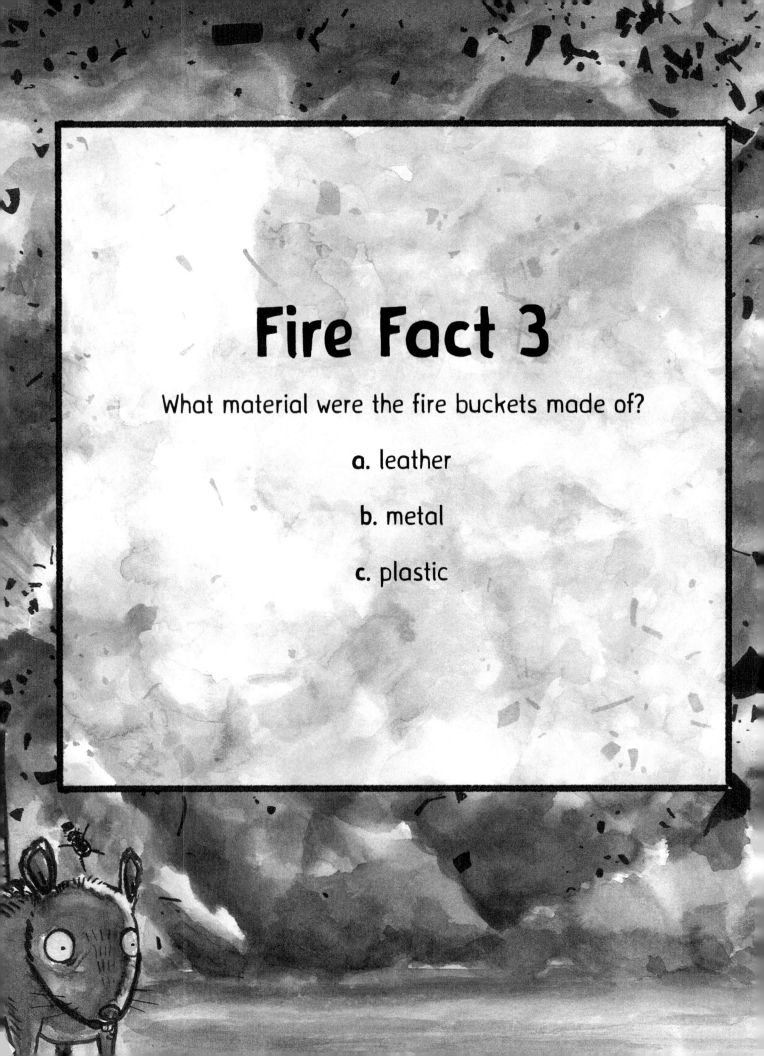

Fire Fact 3

What material were the fire buckets made of?

a. leather

b. metal

c. plastic

St Pauls Cathedral

King Charles II has asked Sir Christopher Wren to rebuild St Pauls Cathedral. He needs some ideas. What do you think the new cathedral should look like? Draw your design below. You never know he might pinch some of your ideas!

Answers

The Great Fire in numbers

On **2nd September 1666** a fire started in the bakery off Pudding Lane. It was **one** o'clock in the morning as the baker, Thomas Farriner and his family escaped from the flames.

The fire burned for **three** days, destroying around **one third** of the City of London. **Thousands** of people carried what they could to the safety of the fields around London where they made shelters.

St Pauls Cathedral was burnt down during the fire. Sir Christopher Wren designed the new cathedral, but it was **forty-four** years before it was complete in **1710**.

What's Wrong?

None of these things existed or lived in 1666.

Who Am I?

King
Charles II

Samuel Pepys

Thomas
Farriner

Firefighter

Soldier

Acrostic

1. **G**unpowder
2. **R**at
3. **E**xplosion
4. **A**sh
5. **T**homas Farriner
6. **F**irehook
7. **I**nferno
8. **R**efugees
9. **E**mbers
10. **O**ven
11. **F**lea
12. **L**eather bucket
13. **O**ne oclock
14. **N**ight
15. **D**aub
16. **O**ut
17. **N**orth

Fire Wordsearch

y	i	g	y	l	i	c	g	b	p	a	d	d	r	o	u	h	c	e	s
n	r	u	b	z	i	h	l	d	s	u	z	e	p	e	f	f	t	f	b
x	u	m	o	n	s	m	o	u	l	d	e	r	n	s	d	i	a	e	l
u	w	l	y	p	h	u	w	m	m	z	j	n	o	u	h	v	c	x	a
s	x	x	c	m	f	f	v	p	o	j	t	w	y	w	h	o	x	k	z
i	l	y	p	f	l	a	m	m	a	b	l	e	l	s	h	r	r	x	e
q	u	y	l	v	i	m	n	n	l	g	c	i	i	w	b	a	s	g	s
o	u	a	g	l	l	n	q	q	i	x	c	a	v	t	l	n	y	d	c
q	r	o	k	c	t	r	m	q	g	t	t	q	s	i	n	g	e	p	t
e	b	l	v	r	z	n	l	o	h	p	r	g	b	u	e	e	a	c	p
v	w	e	m	b	e	r	s	l	t	g	r	o	e	d	m	v	v	q	w
q	t	u	x	i	d	k	l	s	i	s	v	m	s	n	f	z	i	u	k
n	n	x	n	t	s	i	x	e	b	d	k	n	c	q	l	r	x	r	i
b	m	z	f	l	i	c	k	e	r	w	w	p	f	h	a	s	h	l	i
k	u	r	r	a	n	n	h	c	y	c	i	o	i	f	m	f	o	e	n
d	m	m	n	x	q	h	g	r	u	m	j	y	a	b	e	l	l	s	f
h	m	a	e	t	q	y	h	u	b	t	d	x	j	r	s	m	o	k	e
v	w	p	m	p	g	o	u	d	i	p	w	z	j	u	c	y	u	x	r
a	o	g	l	o	t	u	l	s	p	s	x	g	g	z	q	i	n	o	n
w	o	l	l	e	y	n	n	t	i	z	h	i	f	r	e	o	f	u	o

Fire Facts

Fire Fact 1 b. Pudding Lane

Fire Fact 2 c. wine and
Parmesan cheese

Fire Fact 3 a. leather

That's the end of this book, but if you want to read my story you need to get:

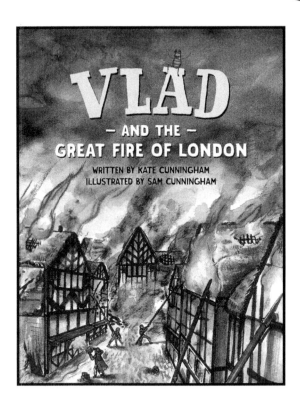

With thanks to everyone who supported us in this venture, especially Sean, Danny and Freddie, who tested all the activities.

Any errors are the responsibility of the author.

This paperback edition published 2017 by Reading Riddle

This edition designed by Rachel Lawston, lawstondesign.com

www.readingriddle.co.uk

ISBN: 978-0-9955205-3-0

For information on further resources and the next Vlad books visit www.readingriddle.co.uk

Printed in Great Britain
by Amazon

85787511R10020